College Daze

Jaylon Moore

Copyright © 2016 by Jaylon Moore

ISBN: 978-1536813814

All rights reserved. No part of this publication may be reproduced, distributed, or transmitted in any form or by any means, including photocopying, recording, or other electronic or mechanical methods, without the prior written permission of the publisher, except in the case of brief quotations embodied in critical reviews and certain other noncommercial uses permitted by copyright law. For permission requests, write to the publisher, addressed "Attention: Permissions Coordinator," at the address below.

Printed in the United States of America

Table of Contents

Acknowledgments (1)

Introduction (3)

Being Greek & Saved (9)

Did I Choose the Right Major? (19)

Did You Really Meet Your Best Friends in College? (31)

Do You Make Time for God? (43)

Love vs. Lust (57)

Conclusion (69)

ACKNOWLEDGEMENTS

Never in a million years did I think I would be given a chance to speak to people about being bold for Christ at a young age. I was reminded that God doesn't care what people think. If he has given you a gift, nobody can take that away. I give glory and honor to my savior, Jesus Christ.

To Cynthia Moore-Hardy, my mother, my main lady, my main critic, but (most importantly) the woman who loves me unconditionally and is my biggest fan, I thank you for every lesson as well as your unwavering love and support! You're the true GOAT (Greatest of All Time). Thanks mom. I love you.

I honor my fathers, Marvin Stewart and Keith Hardy. I thank you for your support and the way you exemplify how a man should be through your actions. I hope to grow up, provide, and love my wife and kids the way you do on a daily basis. I love you both.

To the late Evia B. Moore, I miss you so much. Trying to find a new way of life without you has been difficult. But like you say, there is a lesson in everything. I can hear you saying: "Jaybird, who told you to write a book with them yellow teeth?" And then finishing that statement with "oh say dere now"; smiling all the while. I thank you so much for your prayers. They have covered me and continue to for the rest of my life. I will do my best to uphold the last name, Moore, to the best of my ability. Love you, Nana.

To my grandparents, John and Lillie Hardy; thank you for the delightful blend of laughter, caring deeds, wonderful stories and most of all the love. Grandma Lillie, those words of encouragement that you shared with me in one of the lowest moments of my life, helped me to reach down and pull from my inner strength what I needed to go forward. Thank you and I love you both.

To my family and my best friends, I thank you for your support, accountability, and belief in me. It means a lot to me that you all have remained faithful to me through all of my flaws, and supported my ministry.

I thank my church family, Anderson United Methodist Church. I have the best pastor on this side of the Earth, Rev. Joe May. You all are growing a gladiator in the spirit. I thank the music ministry and the leaders of it. To all of my mentors in the ministry, thank you so much for your teachings. I love you all. Keep me in your prayers as I grow in Christ.

May God bless everyone who reads this book.

INTRODUCTION

The bible tells us in Jeremiah 29:11: " For I know the plans I have for you, declares the Lord, plans to prosper you and not to harm you, plans to give you hope and a future." Growing up, I heard this verse spoken many times. I've always known my creator holds my future in his hands, but I could never really grasp that concept until a year after my first year in college. I spent most of my time in the church. I was a true "pew baby" in every sense of the word. It was so bad that my name was on two rosters for a church. I would attend church with my mom at Anderson United Methodist Church, and then go with my grandmother to Christ Temple Church of Christ Holiness U.S.A. Missing church was not an option in my family. Being caught up in the routine of church, the ministries that came along with it, and the world around made it so that I couldn't see the will of God concerning my life. My parents always taught me to develop a personal relationship with Christ; but because Jaylon was always trying to speak over Jesus, I became lost in the world. It's amazing how God reminds us of who he is and who we are all in one single moment.

Graduating from William B. Murrah High School, I thought I was a pretty cool person. I drove a 2012 peanut-butter-colored Jeep Laredo, formally known as "Legend." I was the head drum major for the band, hung around the coolest people, and talked to one of the prettiest girls in school. On the outside looking in, you would think I had it all together. My plan was to go to Tennessee State University, majoring in "Getting Lit" and minoring in Social Work. When I finally got to Tennessee State, I completely changed my Christ-Like mindset to a worldly one.

In all your ways acknowledge him and he shall direct your path. —Proverbs 3:6

I was acknowledging myself and directing my own path. My plan was going really well, or so I thought. Before I could get good and comfortable, my plan was altered. I came home to Jackson, MS for Labor Day weekend. When I got ready to go back to school, I was in a devastating car accident. The weather as I left Jackson was very bright and as we say on Snapchat, "the lighting was just right."

That moment was too good to be true.

I went a little farther and reached Memphis. As I drove into Jackson (TN), the weather started to look funny. At this point, I was upset because I had to let my windows up, take my shades off, and turn my music down; it looked like it was about to storm, and I had to focus more than I wanted to.

My mom called just then. "Hey how is it going?"

I answered. "It's going good!"

But like any good mother, she could tell that something was bothering her son. "Jay, what's wrong? You sound bothered?"

"I'm really not doing good. The sun just up and left. I had to take my shades off and close my windows."

"Jay, really?"

I told her that I would see her at Christmas as the weather suddenly got really bad. I had to slow down because I don't drive well in the rain. I remember telling my mom that I would have to call her back because I had to focus.

"Okay, take your time. Be safe. I love you."

As soon as I got off the phone, my car jerked really hard. It scared the life out of me! I quickly grabbed my gospel mix cd, put it in, and started praying like I was on the altar. The rain finally cleared up and I was able to get out of Jackson, TN. I praised God for bringing me through the storm. Rain started to come down harder; the wind blew angrily as lightning and thunder filled the skies.

I slowed down again.

Something in my spirit wasn't sitting right.

After twenty minutes, my car jerked again and hydroplaned into the air. My car flew up and flipped and rolled about four times. After the tossing and turning, my car ended up on the right side of the highway on a hill. The car was faced up and I hung outside of the car. When I realized that I had been in a terrible car accident, I started to panic.

It was the worst day of my life!

Blood was everywhere; my windshield was caved in.

Glass was stuck in my face and I started to spit up blood. While the injuries were not severe, I could not shake the traumatic event. Falling to my knees, I called on Jesus. I felt like I was in a nightmare. I didn't know what was going on.

Out of nowhere, a Caucasian man and woman came and picked me up off of the ground. They helped me to relax during that moment. The man and woman called the police, the paramedics, and my parents. I relaxed enough to remember my mother's number. She couldn't really understand that I was in an accident; to her, it sounded like I was dying. My mother and father rushed to Jackson, TN as the ambulance rushed me to the hospital.

So here I am, a freshman away from home sitting in my hospital bed crying because I'm alone. I've neglected God. The flashbacks of the accident replayed in my head. The nurse's sudden appearance distracted me.

"Mr. Moore, what are you doing?"

"Ma'am."

She walked around the hospital bed. "You are a miracle child. Most people don't make it out of accidents like that. You are blessed." She hugged me and prayed. "You're covered and you must fulfill the assignment that's on your life."

I opened my eyes and my parents were walking through the door with a host of family members. I didn't realize that I had closed my eyes until that moment.

Later, as I was leaving, I don't remember seeing the nurse. To this day, I believe she was an angel. She came to me with a warning, of what my life would be if I didn't choose Jesus. She also came with the revelation of what it will be if I choose him.

Have you ever been in a situation where God completely changed your plan? As you can see, my plan turned out to be nothing like the Lord's plan. I believe the Lord was trying to get me to understand that he was still in control of my life and there was nothing I could do or say to stop him from being in control. I learned three important things from this experience: God had a plan for me, always submit to His will, and never become your own God.

"Yet not my will, but yours be done." —Luke 22:42

Do you think I learned from that experience? No!

When I finally realized that I was okay, I gave God praise for letting me live because I wasn't ready to die. My praise was sincere, but all I did was become aware of what God was trying to get me to do: submit completely. However, after all that, I simply wasn't ready to give up doing my own thing. We use that word *simply* a lot, but it's not as simple as it may sound.

I got back to school and went completely wild, doing my own thing with pride. Only this time, I had a full understanding of what God was calling me to do and be. I was embarrassed to talk about some of the stuff I did because it was against my character. The only good thing that came from it was that I maintained a 3.6 GPA.

The second semester came around and I started going

to church. During one particular service, I believe I had my second real encounter with God. After that encounter, I knew that if I wanted to be saved for real and receive everything God had for me, I had to focus on God and nothing else. In college, I have experienced some of the best (and worst) days of my life.

I am in my senior year as I write this, and I am glad that I have made it this far. However, I have a long way to go. Being 21 and saved by God in college is not easy. You have to deal with the pressures of your friends, your major, and your organizations; all of this has to be balanced with your faith. This is a glimpse into my college matriculation and the things I experienced during this season of my life.

BEING GREEK & SAVED

When I considered pledging, I was in the 11th grade. Mentors from my church talked to me about joining Alpha Beau, which is a mentorship program sponsored by the men of the Alpha Phi Alpha Fraternity, Inc. They didn't have it in my area, so I could not join. My friends were talking to me about joining Kappa League, which was sponsored by the men of the Kappa Alpha Psi Fraternity, Inc.

I listened to them and joined because everybody was doing it. Because of all the countless parties and all the females who loved when they shimmed, it was considered cool. Being a part of an organization like Alpha Beau, Kappa League, Sigma Beta, or Omega Gents during high school meant that you were very popular. Everybody wants to be popular in high school, so of course I did it for the popularity.

In the back of my mind, I knew it wasn't for me and I didn't want to be a part of that particular organization anyway. Reminiscing back on the time when I was a part of it, my reluctance probably explains why I missed a lot of meetings, community service events, and parties. It even showed in the way I shimmied, I was horrible. Of course, I wasn't as saved as I am now, so my spiritual walk had no factor in it. The Holy Ghost probably would have told me, *don't do Kappa League.*

During freshman week at Tennessee State, they had an event called "Courtyard" at night. They played music, Greeks strolled about, and people partied. The men of Alpha Phi Alpha Fraternity, Inc. came through out of nowhere, strolling, and I was amazed because I had never seen them in action. I can remember that moment vividly. The words of my mentor ran through my head, "Jaylon, you'll make the right decision when you get to college." It was amazing to be standing at my HBCU, at that moment, watching history and pride showcased in one setting without any problems.

Toward the end of my spring semester as a freshman, my spiritual walk started to increase suddenly. My spirit longed for Christ like never before. From that moment on, I started to be cautious about every move I made. An Alpha from TSU became my mentor during my spring semester, and I remember telling him, "I don't know if it's for me."

His reply resonated with me. "It's not for everybody. Maybe you should do some more studying about the organization."

I did exactly what he said.

I arrived at Jackson State University as a sophomore and the Alphas were getting ready to have forums that educated the campus about the things they were most passionate about as a fraternity. At this point, I was seriously thinking about pledging. Stereotypes of black Greek organizations, the Church's view on pledging, and my view on pledging were going through my mind.

STEREOTYPES

All Greeks do is throw parties. As a whole, they pride themselves on community service, mentorship, educating the community, brotherhood/sisterhood, and advocating for change (when necessary). There are some Greeks who only show up when it's time to party and probably wouldn't mind partying all the time, but this statement is not true for the collective body.

Its members used to be wack or are nothing by themselves. This statement usually comes from people who aspired to be a part of an organization, but for whatever reason could not. Who are you to say somebody is wack? When you are Greek, you stand out amongst the rest; people look up to you and they expect nothing but the best. This doesn't mean that you used to be wack and now you're famous. It simply means that you have a responsibility to people.

Joining a fraternity or sorority does not offer any advantages over other campus activities. When I joined my fraternity, it put me at an advantage compared to many people my age. I can't even begin to describe how many benefits came along with being a part of my fraternity. Job offers, scholarships, and promotions are only a small portion of the advantages that come with being a part of an organization.

All Greeks do is wear paraphernalia and stroll. There are

some Greeks who are just t-shirt wearers. You don't see them out until it's time to hop in line and stroll. They don't show up to any other events, except when it's time to have fun.

THE CHURCH'S VIEW ON PLEDGING

**You shall have no other gods before me.
—Exodus 20:3**

When the scripture above refers to other gods, it's talking about making things your idol. Some people get too consumed in their perspective organizations and before they know it, it becomes their life.

If you pledge, you're going straight to hell (most famous). This is not true. It is sometimes the case that people who pledge neglect God. I have seen this numerous of times. There are some Greeks who have forgotten all about who they are and to whom they belong. They pray just to get what they want and when they receive their membership, they thank everybody but God.

It's too much temptation. There is a lot of temptation in pledging. People who are already in the organization push their views upon you. Spiritual risks are definitely a part of being in a black Greek organization. Based on who you are, spiritual risks are things that drive you away from God's will.

MY VIEW

I'm a man of God before I am anything else. Nothing comes before me and my relationship with God.

**Wisdom is the principal thing; therefore get wisdom: and with all thy getting get understanding.
—Proverbs 4:7.**

Ask a lot of questions. Pay close attention, listen carefully to what the organization says it is, and watch the members of it.

People put emphasis on what they want to put emphasis on and not the whole thing. Look at the whole picture. People put a lot of emphasis on the parties, Greek mess, and strolls. However, they say less about the mentorship, service, and empowerment that Greeks contribute to society.

Do your own research. Don't go off what somebody told you. Do your own research.

It's not for everyone. After you have done your research and asked questions, it may not be for you. You may think you can't commit the time to it or you may be trying to join for the wrong reasons. It's always good to go back and fix your intentions.

Black Greek organizations are not a seasonal organization; it's a lifetime. It's not an undergraduate experience or "when your probate is over, that's it" type of experience. It's a lifetime. Not being Greek doesn't make you less of a person and being Greek does not make you more of a person. If you don't make it in the organization, it doesn't mean that you are a failure. It may not be time for you to become Greek or it may simply not be for you. It can be hard to understand.

On February 14, 2015, I became a part of the Delta Phi Chapter of Alpha Phi Alpha Fraternity, Inc. I remember telling my grandmother what I just became a part of and she was like, "What y'all gone be doing?" Y'all gone be out there stepping and hollin'?"

I laughed. "Yes, we will be stepping and we may holler a couple of times."

"Why y'all got to holler?"

"It represents the pride we have in our organization. Nana, we do more than just step. We advocate for the community. We mentor. We educate our people on drunk driving, college, voting rights, and much more."

Her exact words were, "Be careful, Jay."

"Yes ma'am."

We laughed and talked some more. That was the last time I saw her. She passed the day before my probate on February 28, 2015; I probated on March 1, 2015. For my brothers, this was one of the best days of their life. But for me, it was the worst. I can't even begin to describe the relationship Nana and I had. She was truly a gift from God. My grandmother possessed every quality of a godly woman. Family members on my mother's side didn't know anything about Greek life because the church that they grew up in preached against it. What I learned about Greek life was definitely on my own.

Taking all of these things into consideration as a saved young man who has joined this prestigious organization, do I have anything I would have changed? Yes. When

Nana spoke those last words to me, I knew that meant be strong in who you are, don't waiver, remember what I taught you, and remember who you belong to. I know for a fact I disappointed the promise I made to "be careful." I did not remain firm in abstaining from alcohol and weed; I was drunk and high every chance I could get. I was certainly putting myself at tremendous spiritual risk with the dangerous combination of poor time management, bad spiritual cultivation habits, and subjection to temptation. Exposing my eyes to activities unwholesome to Christians defiled the purity of my heart.

On the other hand, through connections of my fraternity, I'd been pushed closer to God. When I got ready to cross I found my mentor/prophyte and line brother who I connected with had the same longing for Christ that I did. My line brother didn't fall into the same temptations that I did, but he had his own problems. I would often tell him that he was stronger than I was when it came to spiritual risks. When we recognized our mistakes, we became each other's support in order to draw closer to God and to hold each other accountable. After recognizing some of our wrongdoings, we drew closer to God and had more of an impact on our line brothers.

There were two options: conform to what everybody else was doing or speak out about Christ and lead people in the right direction. There were brothers who had not gone to church before and were now coming to church with me; they desired more. It's not just about coming to church. If I can be the light they see which draws them closer to God, then that's good enough for me. Sometimes you are the only representation of Christ that somebody sees; if you're not where God wants you to be, then people will suffer because of your failure to be in His will.

The church as a whole has preached against fraternities and sororities and, in some cases, basically condemned people to hell. They let one person or something the fraternity has done speak for the entire organization. Every organization, including the Church, has one (or several members) who are not a good representation of the organization. It is imperative that we don't let one member of the organization speak for the entire organization. Imagine if the Church had one representative to speak for the body of Christ: nobody would want to come in and be saved. What the body of Christ should do is get people who are saved and Greek to break down the temptations of pledging and share their experiences instead of just saying, "no, don't do this." When I was younger my parents kept me from some things; but as I got older, they didn't just send me out in the wild. They helped guide me through so I could learn how to make wise decisions.

If you are considering pledging, make sure that your intentions are good. Always go back and put your intentions in check. If you know that you are not strong enough to resist the temptations that come with pledging, then don't do it. If you feel like God can use you to draw people closer to him by being in the organization, then by all means do it. If you have no clue why you are doing it, definitely don't do it. It truly is not for everyone. In the words of Nana, "Be careful, Jay."

PRAY THIS PRAYER!

God, whatever organization I join on this earth, let it not come before you. Whether it's a Greek organization or not, I want whatever I do to be pleasing in your sight. Whatever title I obtain on this earth, let it not come before you. You are my first priority and my last resort. I consult you for everything I do. Help me to make the right decisions. I need your guidance and I want to hear your voice more clearly. Father, my thoughts are not your thoughts and my ways are not your ways. I come against the spirit of confusion and bring forth the spirit of truth and the spirit of wisdom. You said in your word that in all thy getting, get an understanding; so I am here, Father, to understand your will for me deeper than I have before. Lord, I'm asking you now that you would send confirmation of your will. Anything that the devil tries to suggest to me, I denounce it now in the name of Jesus. I don't want to be connected to anything that's not going to push me into a more abundant life with you— or help me fulfill my assignment given by you, God. I need you! I don't want to do it without you. I can't imagine my life without you. I surrender my heart, my time, my mind, and my soul; all of it is for you. It is yours. Give me an overwhelming amount of discernment so I will know for sure my next move. In Jesus' name I pray. Amen!

DID I CHOOSE THE RIGHT MAJOR?

I didn't have any direction as to what I wanted to major in during my first year of college. When I was younger, I would always say, "I'm going to be a professional singer and a lawyer." Everybody had thing they wanted to be when they grew up. At age two, things were happening; we were discovering our God-given gifts, and we were dreaming about who we would become. The older you get, the more time makes you start putting dreams into reality. I'm not saying that you stop dreaming, but you have to begin to put words into action. That first year I decided my major would be social work and that I would minor in music. I went back and forth from changing my major from social work to English. Talking to different lawyers, they told me that you can major in anything and still go to law school; however, the best thing to major in was English or political science. I also started to think about majoring in mass communications. I figured I would make a good news anchor.

Was God calling me to be a lawyer?
Was God calling me to be a social worker?
Was God calling me to be a news anchor?

The older I got I started to get *those* questions. What's your major? What are you going to do with that? What law school do you want to go to? What kind of attorney do you want to be? I heard you say you sing: what are you going to do with that? Do you want to teach music? What kind of music do you like? What kind of music do you sing?

Given the stress of those serious questions, I did what any other college student would do: I blocked it all out and let time pass me by. This is the worst mistake you can make. There's only about 4-5 years in your undergraduate education, depending on how long you take. Those first two years are mostly prerequisites: the basic courses everybody has to take. Those last two years are the classes geared toward your major. When students go into their third year without any sense of direction, they start to panic because they don't want to keep doing something they have no passion for.

You may be saying, "That's where I am now."

WHAT DO I DO?

When you reach this point in your college career, it's good to just stop and seek God! Don't stop and take a break from school; instead, take a moment to see what it is God is calling you to do. There are several people I know who dropped out of school because they didn't have a clue about what to do. Others majored in something they didn't want to do and graduated, leaving with a degree they didn't care about. If you drop out, you lose your focus and become lost in the world; some people never return to school. Also, it's important to remember that college is not for everyone. But if you're not going to go, make sure you have a plan. If you simply settle, then you will never reach true happiness.

"True happiness involves the full use of one power and talents." —John W. Gardner.

If you change your major a hundred times, drop out of school, settle by doing something you really don't want to do, or if school is simply not for you, God won't love you any less. The only thing that matters is how God will get the glory out of your life. However, I believe it is an insult to God's creation if you don't fulfill his promises concerning your life.

I had to learn this for myself.

I'm sure every college student has thought about dropping out of school more than once. Before I could switch my major for good, I remember praying really hard and seeking counsel from people I trusted the most. Yes, I could have majored in English, political science, or mass communications, but I chose to seek God before I made a move. This was the best decision I ever made. One of my line brothers shared a quote I never heard before when I was thinking about changing my major:

> "When you're good at something, you'll tell everyone. When you're great at something, they'll tell you."
> —Walter Payton

After I heard this, I started to pay attention to how I made people feel. Most people told me I would make a great preacher, social worker, gospel artist, or minister of music at a church. Before my grandmother passed, I remember conversations with her where she told me I sounded like my grandfather, who was a preacher before he passed. I remember my pastor telling me that I was going to be a preacher. People from high school would tell me that I make them want to pursue God more.

Honestly, I never did think about it in depth until I started to seek God about my future and my assignment to the world. I was hearing this all my life and never paid it any attention. I began to think about it more: If God gets the glory out of me being a gospel artist, preaching the word, being the minister of music at a church, or being a social worker, then why not? I would rather spend my life in full time-ministry, knowing that God would get the glory, than settling just to get by. The question I asked myself was: why hadn't I realized this all along? I guess I knew this, but I was caught up in what people would say, what would be easier, and being fearful of the challenge. I find it amazing how we can talk ourselves out of our purpose simply because of fear and uncertainty.

There are some gifts that God puts in people to shake the nation. It is in this moment where you have to apply radical faith. You have not truly worked for your faith until you are willing to look like a fool for it. When everybody thinks that what you're doing is crazy and impossible, then you know you're using your faith. If you are reading this and you know without a shadow of a doubt that God has revealed something to you, don't waste time doing something that won't bring you ultimate happiness. I'm not the number-one supporter of dropping out of school, but if you have a plan and you know school is not for you: get out. If you know you need to be majoring in something else, and if you heard from the Lord, then stop and follow him.

There is a parable in the bible (Mathew 25:14-30) that talks about how Jesus explains to his disciples about his second return and that no man will know the day nor the hour when he shall return. He breaks it down to them using the parable about talents. Talents during that time were referred to as money. This parable does not represent just economic prosperity, but it challenges the believer to use all the gifts that God has given them. In this parable ,the rich man (master) instructs his servants to use the talents that were given to them until he returns. He tells them that when he returns, he is going to check to see what they did with their talents. He gave each servant a talent according to their ability. To one servant, he gave 5 talents; to another, he gave 2 talents; and another, he gave 1 talent. The one who received a single talent buried it in the ground. This servant was too afraid to take a risk because he didn't understand the unknown. He was also severely punished. Jesus explained to his disciples through this parable that you should use the talents given to you to build the kingdom and use them as if I am returning today.

So my question to you is: what will you be doing when Jesus returns?

Just like Jesus stressed the importance of using talents to his disciples, even now he is stressing the importance to us as believers to use the talents that he has given to us. There are some people who are counting on you. If you sweep the talent that God gave you under the rug, then you will never reach your destiny; you won't please God.

If you're not doing what God called you to do, who are you serving?

The other two servants were faithful, honored, respected, but, most of all, feared the master so much that they didn't want to see what the consequences were if they didn't do what they were assigned to do.

Why is it that we as believers depend, respect, and honor the world more than we do God?

He has given you everything you need to be successful, but you have to trust him—even if it's challenging. This parable is about teaching us accountability. Jesus will soon return and he is going to want to know what you did with the stuff he gave you. Don't waste time worrying about what somebody else has or what they are doing, worry about what God gave you. At the end of the day, you want to hear him say: "well done, my good and faithful servant" and not "depart from me, for I never knew you." When you are operating within what God told you to do, you are building a relationship with him because you have to seek him for every move. When you are not, you are building a relationship with the world and feeding your flesh. The consequence won't be as severe as the servant who buried the talent in the ground, but there will be people who will suffer because they decided not to walk in God's purpose.

Who is it that will be tied up in your disobedience?

It's easier to seek God for his will concerning your life rather than depending on yourself for what you believe is your purpose—or listening to other people about what they think you should do. These are ways to seek God on your major.

Each of you should use whatever gift you have received to serve others, as faithful stewards of God's grace in its various forms. —1 Peter 4:10

Pay attention to how you are wired. Write out some of the things that you do well. Pay attention to the things people think you do well. What are some of things that you are most passionate about? When what people say about you agrees with your passions, and what God has already revealed to you, it can be a solid indication on your God-given purpose. Search yourself for what you believe you can do best to honor God with your life.

Christian advice from spiritual advisors and those you trust.

Spiritual advisors are your pastors, youth pastors, campus ministers, young adult leaders, mama and daddy, mentors, etc. It can be anybody who witnesses your spiritual walk on a daily basis. If you don't have one, I strongly suggest that you get at least one or two. Advisors are good because they help you to discern your spiritual gifts and make sense out of them. They also intercede on your behalf. Talk with experienced employees or employers in your area of choice and ask important questions. How did you determine God's will? If you were to attend college again what would you do differently? Who else would you recommend that I talk to for this type of employment?

Fix your intentions. The #1 goal is to please God so that he can get the glory out of your life. If your intention for being successful is to prove a point to somebody, then your intentions are wrong. Speak blessings over everyone no matter how much they doubted you. If you're trying to major in something where you just want to make a lot of money when you get out of college, your intentions are wrong. Your God-given gifts will make room for you—meaning opportunities and money. In the words of Bishop Joseph Walker: "If it's God's will, it's God's bill." He'll take care of it.

Silence the negative voices. "I can't do this!" "I'm scared!" "What if this happens?" "Am I good enough?" "They're better than me." "How long is it gone take?" "If I do this, it will be easier." The more you keep feeding your spirit with sayings such as this, the quicker you kill your gifts. You don't know what you can accomplish until you actually try. If you know God called you to do something, then he will equip you. Yes, it won't be easy, but you're built for it. Change those voice. "I can do this!" I'm fearless!" "I can't wait for this to happen!" "I am good enough!" "I'm not worried about who's better than me; I'm doing me!"

> **Life and death is in the power of the tongue.
> —Proverbs 18:21**

I was given the opportunity to audition for the background vocalist position for Tasha Cobbs Ministries in Atlanta. Unfortunately, I was not selected. However, the experience was amazing! When you work hard for something, it's not easy receiving a "no," but I had to look at every "no" that I received to be in God's will. Being in a season when you are hearing "no" often is never a good feeling, but it's necessary and you have to keep believing that your "yes" will come in time. Until then, I have to continue to seek God and perfect what he has given to me!

When you really understand what God is calling you to do, nothing will be able to stop you. It took me going all the way to Atlanta, Georgia to receive a "no" in order to break out of fear and the opinions of others. During this experience, I wasn't chasing platforms, money, or fame. All I wanted to do was follow God. So now, when people ask me what I want to do when I graduate, I tell them with no hesitation: I want to go into full-time ministry. When I graduate from college I will be going to graduate school to enter into a dual program to receive my Master's in social work and my Master's in divinity. I want to be a preacher and pursue music ministry full-time.

Usually when God calls you to do something, it's the total opposite of what you were thinking or how you had it planned. I've always wondered what my life would be like if I could play basketball or football, but I'm not blessed with the coordination to play a sport. It's just not in me! There are so many people that try and do things that are just not them. Stay in your lane! God cannot use me in a sport to share his gospel and that's okay. God will equip you with a gift to get your foot in the door in order to make the gospel of Jesus Christ known. It's easy for God to use a basketball player like Steph Curry to share the gospel because he can actually play basketball, and he has something in common with the players. Whatever field your gifted in, use that as your outlet to make Christ known.

Remember: God cannot bless who you pretend to be.

I would have never imagined wanting to be a preacher. It has been confirmed in my pursuit toward God and by several trustworthy preachers of the gospel. I've always thought it was too much responsibility, but you have to learn how to trust God—even in the unknown.

While you may decide on keeping your major (or changing it), consider the following to help you find a good fit between who you are, how the Lord is leading your life, and the major you choose to help you prepare for a Christ-honoring life. Always follow Solomon's example and continue to ask God for discernment. In 1st Kings 3:5-10, the Lord appeared to Solomon in a dream and told Solomon to ask for whatever he wanted. Solomon told the Lord: I am only a little child and I don't know how to carry out all of my duties. He thought about what he didn't have, so he asked the Lord to give him a discerning heart to distinguish right from wrong.

While in college, we often think we are old enough to not consult anybody on the decisions concerning our life. We will always be God's children—and he knows best. God has given us many assignments and it is our job to ask questions if we don't understand. When the teacher administers an assignment and we don't understand, we ask questions so we won't make the wrong decisions.

When it comes down to God, why do we make life-changing decisions without consulting the one who gave us the vision?

He knows the steps to take; all you have to do is follow. Don't waste time on the wrong thing, God has anointed you to accomplish your assignment, but you are responsible for developing your gifts by seeking him. Trust that he is in control and that his word is sufficient to provide direction during this important time in your life.

PRAY THIS PRAYER!

God, forgive me for doing things my own way. Every little thing that concerns my life I'm turning over to you. I want to do whatever is pleasing in your sight. I don't want to die without completing my assignment. Give me the strength to exercise my anointing in the world today. Show me my purpose. Help me to make the right decisions. I cancel out any distractions in the path of doing what you have called me to do. I'm centering my mind on you. I focus my eyes on you. I set my ears to you. I want you to get glory out of my life. Right now, God, I'm praying for strategy. I pray for a game plan, and for the strength and the courage to execute it. I pray that this is the season where I will not be out of place. I'm applying pressure that everything will work in the way you intended it to. Give me the blueprint, show me the sign, and impart wisdom and the spiritual intelligence to walk it out. Holy spirit, show me, teach me, correct me, grow me, and don't let me be drawn away from your plan. Help me to honor the plan that is given by you. I may not understand it all, but I know that it's all working out for my good. In Jesus' name I pray. Amen.

DID YOU REALLY MEET YOUR BEST FRIENDS IN COLLEGE?

Do you meet your *real* friends in college? Some would say yes, but a lot of people would say no; they were really my enemies. I met my best friends while growing up as a child.

Being away from home and meeting new people was not easy at all for me. I knew how to network, but actually connecting with people to build a bond was a struggle. The only friend I had at TSU was my best friend from my hometown. Our parents raised us to make wise decisions, but as freshmen it was still hard to select the right group of friends.

During freshmen orientation at TSU we met a group of people through an organization we joined. Of course, we became a clique and all of the other freshmen followed us. It was exciting at first to be a part of it, but as time went on I learned that some of those people in the clique were not going in the same direction I was.

As time went on, I realized that we were all just friends because of our shared organization.

> **"Everybody that is attached to you is not connected to you."** —Bishop Joseph W. Walker III.

I knew that I had to break ties with some of the people in the clique when the value of true friendship started to break. Here are some signs of a bad friendship:

- Lies
- Stealing
- Skipping class regularly
- Never talking about God
- Drunk driving
- Never encouraging
- Not goal-oriented
- Disrespectful
- They're a liability
- Always feeling used
- Sleeping around with your significant other
- Never trusted
- Don't listen
- Always jealous
- Everything is always about them
- Saying bad things behind your back

None of us are looking to experience these things, but they happen to us all. Just like parenting, there's no rulebook on how to be a best friend; and when people show these signs, they are only acting according to how they have been treated in the past—or what they know. They are still in a position to receive grace because I believe everyone has the capacity to change.

The question is: are they willing?

This is where you draw the line. Anybody can say they want to change their ways, but if they are not willing don't waste time waiting. During my experience of bad friends, I always wondered why I kept attracting bad friends. Looking at that list, I realized that I had been a negligent friend at times. I neglected some of the good friends I had just to be around some people who were bad influences in my life. My mind was set up that if you were not drinking, smoking, or engaging in sexual activity, then your lifestyle was pretty boring. For some reason, I needed to be around people who supported my mess. No, I never said this out loud, but my actions definitely showed it. At that time, following the wrong people was okay to me, but it became old really quick and it delayed some of the things God was trying to do in my life.

Who are you attracting?

I had to set some ground rules for myself so that people I encountered would want to be around me, and I would want to be around them. Setting your ground rules for a strong friendship requires resolute mental toughness.

What are your core values?

This is a good time to write down the things you hold most valuable. As a young adult, there will be a lot of things thrown your way, but you have to stand your ground for the person God is calling you to be. When people come in contact with you they need to know what they will get when they see you. Your response should be: I'm a really cool person, but I go no lower than here. I'm a ride-or-die person, but some things I just don't do and I can't apologize for it.

Half of knowing who you are is knowing who you are not. Who are you?

The worst feeling in life is living life without a purpose. First, you have to understand who God has called you to be in this time.

Before I formed you in the womb I knew you, and before you were born I consecrated you; I appointed you a prophet to the nations. —Jeremiah 1:5

God has already put something in you that makes you, you—and nobody can take that away, not even yourself. So before your mother and father decided to have you, the Lord thought of you and designed an assignment for you to fulfill. Often times, we let what happened to us stop us from knowing who we are, and then we end up becoming something we are not. There are 3 types of people: people who know who they are, people who know who they are but are distracted, and people who don't know who they are.

Which one are you?

People who know who they are. People who know who they are live a fearless life. It doesn't matter to them what the world thinks, what people may say, or how things turn out. The only thing that concerns them is doing what God has called them to do. They understand that they have to be separate from the crowd and that is where we all want to be. It's not easy, but in due time we can get there; trust the process. These are the type of friends who can be considered confidants. They are your ride-or-die friends. They hang in there with you during the good times and bad.

People who know who they are but are distracted. People who know who they are (but are distracted) have a clear revelation of what God has called them to do. The very thing that you are called to do has been confirmed in your spirit; and is something you have probably heard before. Being distracted is what prevents you from walking in your calling and fulfilling your assignment. Distractions come in the form of addictions, stressful relationships, past experiences, a bad group of friends, and being in the wrong place at the wrong time—which shapes your identity and how you operate. What's your biggest distraction and what are ways to prevent it? We are living in a time when you have to pay close attention to what is distracting you and what could potentially distract you from your destiny. Distracted people are friends who can be considered as constituents. Constituents are there for what you're about. They are there for the cause because you share similar goals. They are not there for you; they are there for where you are going. Once they reach their destination, they will leave.

People who don't know who they are. People who don't

know who they are have a desire to know who they are, but don't know the first step to finding that out. They simply just want to be somebody else. People let years of their life go by without ever knowing who they are. These people spend most of their time trying to seek confirmation in people and things that are not good for them. This can be a result of how you were reared as a child—not having someone to properly embrace or acknowledge your gifts and talents. These people seek confirmation in things like Instagram. "How many followers do I have?" "How many likes do I have on my pictures?" They also look at celebrities and try to imitate everything they do because there is no one to show them their worth. Sometimes, it develops into trying to talk, dress, and walk like them. This is not healthy because God has created us all differently to serve him for a specific reason, but you only find that out through seeking him wholeheartedly. Friends who don't know who they are should be considered comrades. Comrades are not for you and not for what you're about. They will hook up with you only because they are against what you are against and they need your help to kill what you're against. Don't get blinded by these people because their ultimate goal is to take you out.

We have all been in one of these categories in our lives at one point or another, and some of us may be there now. This doesn't mean that if you are in one of these positions you can't be changed; everyone's goal is to know who they are so they can be a confidant. I knew who I was, but I was distracted. It's all about how consistent you are with being who you are. If you sway often between following the crowd, wrestling with the opinions of others, and doing everything contrary to the will of God, you will lose your credibility or witness. At some point as Christians, we all lose our credibility.

I recall telling somebody you shouldn't be doing this, but then I found myself leaving church after leading praise and worship to engage in sexual activity—or finding myself posting on social media on how to live holy but my lifestyle is not adding up to what I'm preaching. Nobody has ever told me that I'm hypocritical, but people don't miss anything. Because of that, they are waiting on that moment to say "I told you so, they're not who they say they are."

My cousin and I were having a conversation about how we were just basically living reckless. The conversation continued for days because the stories kept adding up. One day, I wondered what it was going take for us to get it together? My exact words were: "I'm tired. This ain't me—no way." I got to a point where I didn't want to live a double life.

**A double minded man is unstable in all of his ways.
—James 1:8**

One minute I'm over here, the next I'm over there. I had to either love one or despise the other. I was tired of being one of those people on social media who seem like a really cool dude or really saved, but you see me out and it's the total opposite. I want my lifestyle to be an example. This book won't serve a purpose if I'm going to keep being reckless.

People will respect you for being who you are. It's okay to be different, but if you dibble and dabble in everything that looks good but is not good for you, people will lose respect for you. I used to struggle with the opinions of others until I realized that the only reason why they have an opinion is because they have inner struggles themselves. Nobody is perfect! People I thought were perfect, especially Christians, were the main ones "outchea wildin'."

"Don't let the opinions of the average man sway you. Dream, and he thinks you're crazy. Succeed, and he thinks you're lucky. Acquire wealth, and he thinks you're greedy. Pay no attention. He simply doesn't understand." —Robert G. Allen

People will always judge or hate on you in secret. Some do it out loud. They will always question why you choose to live this way and who you are. But they will never know what you had to go through to get to where you are. They will never know who you were before you got saved. They will never know what it took for you to get saved. They don't understand that the joy you have now is because of some pain you endured. They don't understand that the job you have now required a lot of patience and responsibility. God did a new work in me and is doing a new work in you on purpose—and some people just won't understand. Have peace in knowing that you are not the same soul you used to be. A lot has changed. A lot had to change. Even though people will expect to see who you used to be, your true friends should not because what you embodied in the past no longer exists.

There are some people in college you will come in contact with that don't care about you trying to live for God. These types of people only care about 3 things: the lust of the flesh, lust of the eye, and the pride of life. This describes the systems of the world. It is set up to make it seem as if only "this life" is important.

For what shall it profit a man, if he shall gain the whole world, and lose his own soul? —Mark 8:36

As believers we build our hopes on eternal things because this world is not our home. It is a system that comprises a way of life where concerns of the flesh are the norm.

**Be ye not unequally yoked with unbelievers.
—2 Corinthians 6:14**

Most people use this verse to refer to relationships, but it can be used for friendships as well. You have to ask God to surround you with like-minded believers. We cannot associate closely with people who don't live according to the will of God because we risk ending up in places we don't belong, doing things we know we have no business doing. Nothing will be more heartbreaking than when we wake up and realize that we've allowed sin to dim the light within us to the point where there's no longer a difference between us and them.

This is also a struggle for people who are connected through various organizations. Being unequally yoked with unbelievers applies wherever you go. We've heard the saying plenty of times before, "Everybody in the church is not saved." This is true and just like everybody in the church not being saved, everybody in a fraternity/sorority, job, student government association, or church is not saved. You are not obligated to be best friends with somebody because they are a part of your organization. It's hard for people to accept that and you might be misunderstood sometimes. They might call you stuck up. They may even run your name into the ground, but you have to understand that everybody is not going where you're going.

If you choose to be saved, this does not mean that you are a better person or a better friend than other people of the world. It simply means that you are trying to live for God completely. I meet people all the time who are saved, and all day long they criticize people who are not. If you see them in church, they are speaking in tongues; but if you see them out in person, they can't even say hello. There's a difference between hanging out with somebody and being cordial to people when you see them. As Christians we have to learn how to be the example instead of beating people up with our words and facial expressions because, truthfully, we were just like them or worse. It's only because of grace and mercy that we are still standing today. You don't have to be somebody's best friend to be an example; they will know you are a Christian by your love. Make friends with people who are going where you are going and that will propel you into your purpose. You won't truly value a good connection until you've experienced a bad one.

Some people are connected for your purpose; others are connected for your demise (your termination).

Discern the difference.

I can honestly say when I started being the friend that I wanted to attract, my real friends came. Not too many people were added to my circle because I didn't need a really big circle. I always thought that if you had 10 people or more in your inner circle and you all call each other best friends, then somebody is not telling the truth. God truly perfected this area of my life and put me on track. When He connects you with people that is called a divine connection, and you will know because you all will be on one accord all of the time. Some people will never see themselves where God sees them. It came to a point where I don't want to be friends with somebody who doesn't want to be anybody. I don't want to go with somebody who is not trying to go anywhere. Divine connections will push you into your destiny. Seek these kinds of connections instead of worldly connections. One propels while the other one hinders. God is seeking to connect you with people. Let him!

PRAY THIS PRAYER!

Lord, help me to be grounded in you no matter what. Strengthen my spirit to be strong in you when temptation arises in my life. You said in your word that if I resist the devil, he will flee. So now, God, I'm turning my ways over to you. I'm on the battlefield for you and I will fight with everything I have. You are my firm foundation. A rock in a weary land. A shelter in a time of trouble. And because of that I cling to the rock of my salvation. At times it seems as if I'm in this fight alone, but I know you are here. Even though I can't see you, I still trust you. It's through you that I build my trust. Protect me from anybody who is not sent by you. Help me to be the friend I want to attract. God, only you can break friendships that are not beneficial for me and not connected to my purpose. In the name of Jesus, I break any connection that is not in the will of God. I break it and I don't want to return to it. Show me, God, the people in my life who are here for me. Help me to honor them, love them, and support them better. Right now, God, I intercede for my true friends, asking that you will cover our friendship. Show yourself strong in our lives so that we may conquer the enemy and any force that tries to come against what you put together. Thank you, Father. In Jesus' name I pray. Amen.

DO YOU MAKE TIME FOR GOD?

As young adults, we neglect God the most! We are so young and have so much going on that we forget about him. It's hard to miss a "turn up" to go to church. How can we say we love God, but we don't spend time with him? Sadly, I was one of those people. Depending on who I was around you would think I had a good relationship with God, but I really didn't. I realized that a lot of people think they have a relationship with God because they are nice people, they go to church, they pray occasionally, or they work in the church.

True enough, I prayed.

True enough, I attended church on the regular.

True enough, I was actively involved in the church, but I didn't have a personal relationship with God. If I would have died, God probably wouldn't even know my name. I had to realize that it's not enough to know the Jesus of my grandmother, mama, daddy, pastor, minister of music, cousin, or mentor. I have to know Jesus for myself. Will I know what they have taught me when they are all gone?

They can't save me a seat in heaven; I can only reserve

my own. I had more quality time with my flesh than I did with God. I did every little thing that supported my plan and my own way of living. It was so bad that I couldn't discern between what was wrong and right. What I thought was right was wrong, and what was wrong was right.

I couldn't hear God at all.

There are no words to describe this.

I was lost!

It was because I didn't know God. Something had to change in my life. Nothing was satisfying me. It was all about Jaylon, Jaylon, Jaylon. What drew me back to the right relationship was me crying out to God. I told God I'm lost and I need a savior because my way is not working. When everything in your life seems like it's failing or you're not being satisfied, it's because nothing else satisfies you but God. I promised him that I would never leave his presence and from that moment I have never left his side.

You can learn something about God every day by spending time with him. I heard so many good and bad stories about what people thought God was like. Nothing beats learning and experiencing for yourself who He is. It changes how you see the objections for people who do know Him as you know Him. When you encounter Him for yourself, you will know Him better and no one will be able to tell you otherwise. If somebody tells you something different about who God is, then they don't know him; he doesn't change and his word is true.

**Jesus Christ is the same yesterday today and forever.
—Hebrews 13:8**

The two things to know about God are:

God is Love. John 3:16—For God so loved the world that he gave his only begotten son that who so ever believe on him shall have ever lasting life. The very nature of God is love. As people, we can choose who we love or where we show love. Love is not something He chooses to give or do, but it's the very essence of Him. It motivates His every action, directs His activities, and reflects His desires. The focus of God's love is redemption. There is no action so wrong, place so bad you cannot go, or situation so bad you can get yourself into that the love of Christ can't save you. His love is unconditional and unfailing. That simply means that it endures until the ends of the earth. When Jesus died on the cross, he stepped in between the law and the people. If we really got what we deserved, some of us would not be here—but he justified us even in our wrongdoing. His sacrifice on the cross says that I know that they are wrong, I know that they make mistakes, I know that they may do things that are not pleasing, but my blood will speak on their behalf. He loves every flaw about us; and when it seems like nobody else does, he still loves us. He loves us so much that he is not ashamed to be identified with the parts of us that we think we need to hide. This is the love of Christ.

God is holy. It's just something about being a child of God. To be holy is to be righteous or just. This means nobody can mistreat you and get away with it if you have your faith in God. Anything that is wrong God will surely make it right. God is a god of justice. The main idea behind holiness is separation. He is perfect in all of his ways and because of that, sin or any evil force cannot operate in his presence. As believers, we are commanded to be holy, as he is holy. This doesn't make believers perfect because of this commandment, but it is a standard that we abide by and strive toward daily. Holiness describes the fear of God. When you fear God that means you have enough respect for him to turn away from all of your wicked ways. Your personal relationship is priority; if that's in place, everything else will prosper. Quality time consists of prayer, praise and worship, studying his word, and going to church.

PRAYER

The breakfast of champions is prayer. Prayer is the way we communicate with God and how God communicates with us.

Be careful for nothing; but in everything by prayer and supplication with thanksgiving let your requests be made known unto God. —Philippians 4:6

He gets to know us better through prayer. This is a spiritual weapon you have to get serious about. Praying a ten-cent prayer expecting a million-dollar answer will not help you at all. "Lord lay me down to sleep, I pray the lord my soul to keep" or "Thank you, Lord, for another day" type prayers won't strengthen your relationship with God. It is okay if you don't really know how to pray. There's not a rulebook that shows people how to pray. As a matter of fact, it's really not even taught in church. A lot of people look for other people to pray for them, and this can be good and bad. The good part is that they may have a good relationship with God—and they may truly be genuine in their prayer for you. Then there are other people who will intentionally pray against you. Don't depend on people to pray for you! When you pray, be in the spirit—intentional and transparent. There would be times when I prayed and my mind would not truly be on God. Everything else would be distracting me from my time with God.

God wants your undivided attention. That's why you have to pray in the spirit because it's the spirit that makes intercession for you. When you are in the spirit, the devil cannot understand what you and God are talking about. You begin to pray for things YOUR will would have missed.

In the same way, the Spirit helps us in our weakness. We do not know what we ought to pray for, but the spirit himself intercedes for us through wordless groans. —Romans 8:26

Basically, God understands our every moan, our deepest cry and screams. You have probably heard the saying, "Be careful what you pray for because you just might get it." Being intentional about what you pray for is key to your next level. You can't pray for a house when you can't even take care of your apartment. You can't pray for a car, or a new car, when you can't even pay tithes and take care of the car you have. You can't pray for a relationship when you don't know who you are yet. This is not to discourage you from praying for the things that you want God to bless you with. God wants to bless you with the desires of your heart, but you first have to be intentional about God working on your heart; to make sure it's right so you can handle what he blesses you with. Transparency with God is understanding that there is nothing about you that God doesn't know. That's the time to cry out to God and tell him what you're dealing with, where you need guidance, and repent all of your sins.

Repent, then, and turn to God, so that your sins may be wiped out, that times of refreshing may come from the Lord. —Acts 3:19

When you are transparent about the things you have done wrong and you confess it, God wipes it away forever. This is also a time to love on God. Tell him how good he is and thank him for the things he has done, is doing right now, and is going to do. Praying like this requires discipline. You have to literally train yourself every day to pray like this in the morning when you wake— and especially at night. Sometimes, it's good during the day to get some quiet time with just you and God to pray.

> "Don't pray when you feel like it. Have an appointment with the Lord and keep it. A man is powerful on his knees." —Corrie Ten Boom

PRAISE AND WORSHIP

When most people think of praise and worship, they think of the songs sung before church really gets started. Some think of praise being a fast song that you jump all over the place and worship being a slow song that's long and drawn out. As leaders in music ministry, we have failed the church by making others think that it's just about a song. Now don't get me wrong, praise and worship can be sung and played by musical instruments, but it's not limited to just that. Praise is simply saying "thank you, God" for the things he has done for us and telling others about the goodness of God. My favorite example of praise is shown in the book of Acts in the Bible.

**And at midnight Paul and Silas prayed, and sang praises unto God: and the prisoners heard them. And suddenly there was a great earthquake, so that the foundations of the prison were shaken: and immediately all the doors were opened, and every one's bands were loosed.
—Acts 16: 25-26**

Paul and Silas prayed and praised so hard that God favored them and everybody around. Praise has the ability to be that strong. The power of praise can open doors in your life that have been shut and break chains that have been crippling you and anybody connected to you. Just like the devil does now in your daily struggles. He tries to make you stop praising God when things are going bad. Sometimes, it's difficult to praise God when things aren't looking good, but that's when you praise the most. When you get in your mind that no matter what you're going through God is still worthy of the praise, that's when what you're looking for is going to manifest itself on Earth.

Worship is defined by the priority we place on who God is in our lives and where God is on our list of priorities. It is truly a matter of the heart. Worship is a lifestyle!

Therefore, I urge you, brothers and sisters, in view of God's mercy, to offer your bodies as a living sacrifice, holy and pleasing to God, this is your true and proper worship. —Romans 12:1

Only when our minds are changed from being centered on worldly things to being centered on God can we worship in spirit. Any type of distraction can flood our minds as we try to praise and glorify God, which hinders our true worship.

God is spirit, and his worshipers must worship in Spirit and in truth. —John 24:4

God has revealed his truth to us through his word.

When I was younger, I used to sing all over the house. Sometimes, I would get very loud and it was very annoying to the people in the house. Before my mom got married, it was me, my mother, and grandmother in the house. My mom says the reason why I sing is because she used to sing to me in the womb. I would spend extra time in the bathroom just to sing; it was my happy place. When my mom got married to my stepdad, we all moved in together.

My daddy woke up one morning and said, "Does he sing like this in the morning, too?"

My mom replied, "Yes, he has been doing it all of his life."

I was only 6 then. He couldn't understand why she allowed me to wake up the house with singing. My daddy soon got used to it. He says that I get it from my mama because she walks around the house and sings as well. He felt like it was a church service at home. I'm so glad that my mama didn't shut me up. The older I got, I realized that what I was doing was building my war room. Even at the age of 6, I was making time for God. Now that I'm older, no matter how I feel, or what's going on, I still find time for God and sing his praises.

Worship will get you through the roughest times in your life because it shifts your focus from the problem to the problem-solver. Worship for me doesn't start when I get to church or when I grace a stage to sing; it starts at home. It's in my personal time with God where I hear him the most. My prayer life has increased. My gift has increased, and God has revealed secret things to me in that special place concerning my life that I would not hear unless I was there. So when people ask me where am I most happy, I tell them in my bathroom (my war room).

Going to church is good. Attending Bible study is great. Developing small groups is wonderful. Being a part of a campus ministry will carry you a long way. But being alone with the one that you pursue, who in return pursues you, is the only thing that matters.

Let this lifestyle overtake you.

I still believe that private time with God brings about the greatest change and reward. You will not regret this. To be honest, this is what's keeping me alive.

STUDYING GOD'S WORD

You must have God's word to live right and to fulfill your purpose.

All Scripture is breathed out by God and profitable for teaching, for reproof, for correction, and for training in righteousness, that the man of God may be complete, equipped for every good work. —2 Timothy 3:16-17

One word can change your life forever. The word of God creates faith, defeats temptation, builds character, cleanses our mind, heals hurt, produces change, and secures our future. We will never be able to experience this if we don't read his word. His word is essential; you cannot live without it. Your next level depends on how much word you have in you. Read the word, learn the word, and act on the word.

GOING TO CHURCH

We live in a culture where millennials think going to church is irrelevant. Some of us were born and raised in the church—and, for whatever reason, we don't go. When I ask people why they don't go to church anymore, the first thing they say is that the love is not there, too many people are worried about how I look, I was hurt in the church, I don't feel like going, I have other stuff to do, I can have church at home, and the truth is not preached anymore. I can identify with those people who don't feel loved at the church.

At some churches, the love is simply not there.

Depending on where you go, there are still some people who are overly concerned with what you have on your body. Instead of teaching modesty, they look at you funny. It doesn't matter if you are at church or at home; if you live long enough, people will hurt you. Not feeling like going to church is a sorry excuse. Having other stuff to do is another sorry excuse for you simply not wanting to go. Churches are always working around the schedules of people—even throughout the week. Yes, you can have church at home and church can even be in your heart, but there are some blessings that you will only receive by being at the church. The authenticity of churches has diminished over the years, and the attention of everything else is more important than Jesus. But there is a church out there for you who has your best interest at heart so you can encounter Jesus like never before.

When you become a young adult, you are experiencing

a different devil than you did when you were a child or teenager. Mama and daddy are not there to keep you on track and feed you the word; it's all on you now. This is why you have to find a church that is preaching and teaching the word of God—where it is correcting you, but also giving you hope. You need a church where you can feel the love and not just hear about it. Find a church that has a relevant word for your life. Seek after a spirit-filled church that is preaching holiness rather than a watered-down, playing-it-safe church that leaves you empty and struggling with the same sins. A church like this is possible, as all churches are not the same. Church will strengthen you on how to read the word so you won't believe everything that comes out of somebody's mouth. Most young adults aren't strong enough to stay at home and read the word. Going to church provides you with opportunities to learn His word better and more fluently. Opportunities such as small groups, Bible studies, and different ministries provide you with the tools that will strengthen your spirit.

God wants you to enjoy your youthfulness, but don't set yourself up for failure by enjoying your youthfulness and forgetting about the one who gives you life. I used to think if I were to sell out to God, I would miss something. You are not going to miss anything. He is a jealous God and He wants to spend time with you. He's just saying, "Don't forget about me."

PRAY THIS PRAYER!

God, I'm sorry! There are so many things that have my attention. I have neglected my first love. I have loved people who don't love me back. I have worshipped people who I should not worship. I have praised people who I should not praise. And the one who loves me, the one who pursues me, the one who picks me up when I fall, I have abandoned.

God, I'm giving you my full attention! Take over my life. Help me to learn more about you through your word. Help me to give you a fresh worship and a fresh praise. I want to communicate with you deeper in prayer. Increase these areas of my life.

God, help me find my way! Live in me, God. I'm at a place in my life where I'm not looking for a visitation; I'm looking for you to live in me. Take over my mind: I want to think like you. Take over my heart: I want to love like you. Take over my mouth: I want to talk like you. Take over my ears: I want to hear like you. Everything in my life that seeks more attention than you, I denounce it now.

You are the only thing that matters.

In a world that's forever changing, you remain the same; so I consciously pursue your presence. It's in your presence where I find who I really am. It's in you that I live, move, and have my being. I'm a lost cause without you. As the deer pants for the water, so my soul longs after you. No longer will I let anyone else fill the thirst of my soul. They have failed me every time. I'm running back to you with everything I got. I'm begging you.

Please forgive me! I need you in my life. I'm not letting you go! Thank you for calling me back into the right relationship with you! In Jesus' name I pray. Amen.

LOVE VS. LUST

Relationships are what most young adults look forward to in college. I remember hearing about the ratio of women to men my freshman year at TSU, it was 10 to 1. At JSU, it was 4 to 1. As a graduating senior in high school going into college, I would hear things like, "it's so many hoes in college," referring to females who don't mind having sex.

"Jaylon, you better get you a box of condoms." In other words, you're going to be having a lot of sex, so prepare yourself so you won't get a girl pregnant. "Jaylon, don't love these hoes." This means don't build a relationship with them; only use them for sex.

Hormones are at an all-time high during this time.

According to Erikson's 8 stages of Development, young adulthood ranges from 18 to 35 years old. This is the age range where we seek deep intimacy and satisfying relationships. Before we can even think about deep intimacy and satisfying relationships, we have one thing that has been killing relationships for years.

It's the spirit of lust!

There is a difference between love and lust.

The root of relationships nowadays is lust.

SIGNS OF LUST

Focus more on the outside than inside. Looks are the only thing that matters. The only thing you are looking at is how big her booty is or how much of a six pack the man has. It's not what's on the outside that will carry the relationship far; it's what's on the inside.

Skipping the friend stage. Don't skip this stage of a relationship. When you are involved with somebody and you jump into their skirt/pants before you jump into their head, this is a sign of a bad relationship. Ask questions. What are their goals? Where are they from? Do they believe in God? Are they saved? Where do they see themselves in 10 years? What's their major?

Your memories are associated with the bed alone. The only memories you have of your relationship is having sex with each other. If the only thing you can remember about your relationship is the first time you had sex, the time you all got caught, almost got caught, the time you snuck into their dorm room, or when you all had sex in the car, then you are definitely not in love; you're in LUST.

No plans for the future. If the woman or man does not have any intentions regarding the relationship, then it's lust. God is not the author of confusion; the devil is.

Doesn't know how to pray. If you are in a relationship and you can't pray for one another, it's not a relationship. If you ever want to know what kind of relationship you are in, ask the person you are in it with to pray for you. You'll see.

Lust doesn't start in college.

Sexual desires are natural and they are tied to our spiritual person. Our spirit is made to desire physically and spiritually the love of another individual. It is okay to appreciate the spiritual and physical beauty in another. What has to be understood is when those desires turn from being healthy to unhealthy. You can't let those desires overpower and enslave you. When you were younger, you probably could not explain some of the feelings you were having, and the first thing somebody said was DON'T HAVE SEX or WAIT TIL MARRIAGE instead of helping you process what was going on. In most cases those "negatives" come from people in the church that have been "outchea." I refer to those people as people who faked their deliverance because they are not strong enough to help somebody else learn from their mistakes.

If you're delivered, you're free to talk about it.

The only way you overcome is by the blood of the lamb and "THE WORDS" of your testimony. If you tell somebody "no" all the time with no explanation, they are more susceptible to doing it, but if you explain what's going on, they are able to make wise decisions. The older you get, the wiser you become. Just like food, no matter what you do, you will always feel hunger in your life. However, you can control how much you eat. You can't stop a bird from flying above your head, but you can stop him from building a nest on your head. You can't stop your sexual desires, but you can stop those desires from being a sin.

"The SIN isn't in FEELING it. It's in FULFILLING it."
—Tye Tribbet

Like most male college students, when I got to college I was dealing with the spirit of lust before I started school. All I can remember is that everything people were telling me about college and females was true. It wasn't until I was in church in Nashville that I heard two phenomenal speakers come and speak about relationships. Devon Franklin and Meagan Good came to Mt. Zion Full Gospel Baptist Church Fellowship, and they were talking about how God wants the best for you. Devon Franklin used the verse:

Then Jesus said to his disciples, Whoever wants to be my disciple must deny themselves and take up their cross and follow me. —Matthew 16:24

The more I focused on the verse, I realized that Isaiah 55:8 was right: "For my thoughts are not your thoughts, neither are your ways my ways," declares the Lord. What I want is not what's best for me. The father knows best. It may seem hard to wrap your mind around, but it's true because the spirit of lust can take you out. I know this for a fact because there are some activities that I engaged in because of the spirit of lust. It robs you of your wisdom and you won't be able to hear from God. Lust can drive you from having a weakness to being wicked. Weak people know what's right and they may fall into lust by distractions or failure to stay in the will of God. Wicked people began to advocate for the spirit of lust because they have been doing it for so long that it has become habit—and that's all they know.

If I can be honest for a minute, I've been weak to this spirit several times before. There's a story in particular that I share with young adults about how I became weak to this spirit. I was out of town for an event and I hadn't done anything sexually in a long time. My goal was simple: get some. I was standing outside the club and I couldn't get in because I was 20.

There was this girl standing outside with me. She turned to look at me. "What are you getting ready to do?"

"Go back to my car and chill."

"Cool. Can I come?"

"Yeah, come on."

When we got in the car, I found a liquor bottle that I did not finish before going into the club. We sat in my car, talking and drinking the rest of the bottle. By the time we were finished drinking the bottle, we were both drunk. I don't know how I drove to my cousin's apartment and I don't remember how I got in. The following morning I woke up with 4 hickeys around my neck and my shirt on backwards.

This was one of the wildest things I have ever done!

When I woke up and realized what had happened to me, I was very disappointed in myself. Here I am, out of town, and I have completely showed out. I could only think: this is not me at all. I'm not that dude who sleeps around. My mama raised me better than that.

What if I got her pregnant?

What if I caught a disease?

I could have killed somebody driving drunk. What if this? What if that? At this point, I knew that I had become a victim of the spirit of lust. Lust had me thinking a way that was contrary to who I was.

Another example of this is Tyler Perry's *Temptation*. It's the story of Judith and Brice, a married couple who has known each other since they were six years old. The wife is a therapist at a matchmaking agency. She encounters a wealthy internet entrepreneur who wants to invest in the company that Judith works for. Judith is dissatisfied with her job and wants to start her own marriage-counseling business, but Brice tells her to wait until they are more financially stable. Judith works late with Harley (internet entrepreneur) to discuss matchmaking surveys. Harley tells her that his sex life is boring. Judith questions her sex life and tries to improve it with Brice. As Brice's attention to his wife decreases, Harley's increases and he seduces Judith. They go on a trip orchestrated by her boss and Harley has sex with Judith on his private jet. Harley demands that Judith leave her husband. When she leaves her husband, she returns to the house while her mother is there; Harley disrespects her mother. Judith is outraged by this and Harley beats her. Brice is having dinner with his co-worker, Melinda, and he finds out that Melinda has been running from Harley, from whom she contracted HIV. Brice breaks into Harley's place to find Judith beat up in the bathroom and he pulls her out. The story ends with Brice getting a divorce and Judith contracting HIV.

As you can see, Judith was so consumed with the spirit of lust that she left her husband for another man, let a man beat her, disrespected her mother, and ended up with AIDS. It overtook her life FAST! It robbed her of her wisdom and it drew her to doing things she probably thought she would never do. Harley was wicked! He was used to seducing women and destroying their life. Harley was an advocate of the spirit of lust because he was too comfortable in seducing Judith. The product was not selling itself; he was selling it.

This is why you must develop a discerning spirit for people that come in your life because they will seduce you into a different world. It doesn't matter how strong you think you are, the devil does not discriminate. Judith and I were both overtaken by lust. We both risked our lives, but the only difference was: she lost her husband and ended up with HIV. This is nothing to play with because you never know how your story will end up. For me, it took one drunk night to fall completely weak to lust.

What will it be for you?

Stop while you're ahead!

How do you get rid of this spirit? Let's make one thing clear: the flesh will always be the flesh. You will always be attracted to what you're attracted to. The Church has taught that once you are delivered or you're saved, your flesh (things of the world) doesn't desire things of the world anymore.

> **Saying, Father, if thou be willing, remove this cup from me: nevertheless, not my will, but thine, be done.**
> **—Luke 22:42**

As Christians we have heard this verse so many times, but we don't focus on it. You still have a will that's contrary to God's best intentions for you. Just because you decided to follow Christ doesn't mean that certain sins don't look good to you anymore; it just means that what you used to do, you don't do anymore for the love of Christ. The challenge of following God's will is when the very thing that excites your flesh comes around and you still follow God.

> **And He said to me, My grace is sufficient for you, for My strength is made perfect in weakness. Therefore most gladly I will rather boast in my infirmities, that the power of Christ may rest upon me. Therefore I take pleasure in infirmities, in reproaches, in needs, in persecutions, in distresses, for Christ's sake. For when I am weak, then I am strong. —2 Corinthians 12:8-10**

Watching porn, certain people you follow on social media, some people you surround yourself with, the music you listen to, and what you drink. All feed into your desires, and before you know it, your desires become sinful. You may be saying this is a lot to think about, or I don't know if I can do this, but it's the little things that count. I can't keep watching "Porn Hub" and expect to not want to do what I see in a porno. I can't keep following lustful pages (@bigbootydimes or @twerkfetish) that post lustful things on social media just for "thirst traps" and not expect to get trapped. I can't keep spending a lot of time around the people that I know "Gone Go" if I want to be better. I can't keep listening to "Meeting in My Bedroom" every day if my goal is to stop those daily meetings. I can't keep drinking "Hennessey" if I know "Hennything can happen." You know what arouses you and because you know yourself, you have to guard yourself.

Purity requires a fight. We must intentionally feed our eyes and minds with godly things so we don't sit and meditate on the toxic thoughts the enemy will feed us.

I'm a living witness that if you follow God and trust his plan, He will give you the desires of your heart. It's okay to wait for something God sent and not settle. Waiting gives you time to focus on who God is calling you to be. Focus on what really matters: school, family, and your gifts. Those are called the things that make you, you. When you are waiting, you have to trust his timing because it's perfect. If you find yourself rushing, you will make the wrong decisions. During the time when I was making wild decisions, I had to remind myself that if God were to send me the one he had for me, I would completely blow it.

MEN

Stop trying to keep up with your boys. Grow up and do what God called you to do. We can't say we want godly women and then pursue women entertaining our hormones. Who you follow, the conversations you keep, and the girl you go after shows what is really in your heart. Choose to follow Jesus and let him lead you to a virtuous woman. Attracting the woman God has for you is being on fire for God.

Husbands, love your wives, just as Christ loved the church and gave himself up for her. —Ephesians 5:25

Gain control over your sex drive. A man will go through hell and high water for a woman he loves. Even though we live in culture where it's absurd for a man to have control over this, he will defy all odds for the woman he loves.

WOMEN

You have to learn to submit to God before hopping into relationships. Marriage requires unconditional love, constant forgiveness, and a lifetime of learning how to treat someone better than you'd treat yourself. If all you want is sex or pictures for social media, you may not be ready.

Looks alone can't sustain relationships; fix your lifestyle. You're fine, but how is your spiritual walk?

Stop trying to raise a boy. You will waste your time if you don't let him grow up on his own. It's one thing to love who someone is; it's another thing to love who someone can be.

Ladies, if you give "it" up on the first night, then you

are building your relationship off sex, and that's all the dude will want.

Not everyone is mature enough to handle this type of waiting. Some people will have to see on their own just how bad they need God to grow in this area. When God knows you're ready for the responsibility of commitment, he'll reveal the right person under the right circumstances.

Wait patiently!

Don't waste time searching and wishing. Grow and be ready. God will give you a love story far better than one you could dream of. It is my prayer that whatever you do, you don't let lust overtake your life; instead, I hope you choose to let God direct your relationship status. It's all in his perfect plan; when it's over you will be glad you followed him instead of a man.

PRAY THIS PRAYER!

Father, you know my weakness. You know where I struggle the most. You know the things that I am most ashamed of. You see the depths of my heart and you love me all the same. My bad decisions aren't without consequences, but in the frame of your grace, they're never beyond redemption. It amazes me that you still accept me after all the wrong I have done. It amazes me that you still allow me to approach your throne of grace even though I don't deserve it. I'm living in a world where they see me for what I used to do, how I used to talk, what I used to say, and where I used to go. You see me for who you created me to be. With everything I have, God, I'm trying to be everything you called me to be.

God, show me the way!

Help me to discern between the things that may look good to me but are not good for me. I'm praying for double the focus concerning your will for me. Keep my eyes clean, keep my mind clean, and keep my hands clean. You alone have the power to make me pure again!

In the name of Jesus, I denounce all soul ties that have been attached to my life. God, this culture is addicted to instant gratification, the quick hook-up, and the overnight sensation. Help me to defy what the world presents as real love. I want to love how you love, God.

Teach me! I'm willing.

God, if you're not in my relationship, then I don't want to be in it. Help me to break away from any relationship that is not godly. Show me, God, what it really means to be single. Show me how to prepare for a relationship. If it means to spend more time learning about myself and letting some things go, I'll do it. Whatever it takes to stay in your will, show me the way. I am willing and ready. In Jesus' name I pray. Amen.

CONCLUSION

Maintaining your faith will not be easy. God is not going to let the enemy know your next move if you walk in your faith. The devil is trying his best to get you to stop your pursuit toward God at this age. If you ever find yourself slowing down, you are deliberately leaving the devil room to creep in and take away everything you have worked so hard for.

Blessed is the man who remains steadfast under trial, for when he has stood the test he will receive the crown of life, which God has promised to those who love him.
—James 1:12

Everybody wants the promise, but nobody wants the process. Expect to get hit! Whatever it is the devil hits you with, take the hit, but don't stay down! Get back up and try again! No! Getting hit doesn't feel good! But when you keep pressing toward God with everything you have, you are proving to God: yes, I'm knocked down, but I love you more. As a matter of fact, if I just give in, it will all be better, but I love God more! You have to declare that over your life.

I love God more!

It may sound boastful to brag on yourself, but every

now and then you have to encourage yourself. Tell yourself I have what it takes! I'm stronger than this! I'm still winning!

When your spirit grows tired of dealing with the stress of being a young adult, that simply means that your faith is being pushed to the peripheral. This moment in your faith is critical because God is now trying to stretch you and push you closer to the promise he has for your life. It is imperative that you are aligned with his will so that you can meet your destiny on time. I'm sure that everybody can attest to the fact that they have missed some opportunities simply because they were not in the right place at the right time; they were not aligned with the will of God. The timing patterns of life demand our complete trust and dependency on God.

In football, there is a play called the timing pattern.

The wide receiver breaks from the line of scrimmage with his back turned toward the quarterback. Both the quarterback and wide receiver know the pattern. Let's put ourselves in the play. God is the quarterback and you are the wide receiver. It is imperative that you listen to God's daily instruction so you can be in sync with his plays; it is necessary for being in the center of His will. The defensive back already knows the play because he has studied the timing pattern. There are people who have seen how far you've come and they are waiting on you to quit. These individuals are studying your every move—and they are waiting until the time is right for them to come in and take you out. The defensive back is allotted one hit at the line of scrimmage. It is considered a legal hit at the line of scrimmage, but it is designed to take you off your route. If you are a good receiver, you will take the hit and keep going. The hit will not kill you; it will only strengthen you so you can be prepared for the catch. While the receiver's back is turned toward the quarterback, the quarterback then gets ready to throw the ball. The receiver has to know what's going on because the quarterback is getting ready to throw the ball to a spot on the field instead of the receiver's hands.

You must understand now: the devil is extremely nervous because he knows that eyes haven't seen, ears haven't heard. Neither has it entered into the hearts of man, the things which God hath prepared for them that love him. So he is thrown off his game because he doesn't know what's to come. God has already released your promise into the atmosphere and it is set to land at a certain spot.

For no matter how many promises God has made, they are "Yes" in Christ. And so through him the "Amen" is spoken by us to the glory of God. —2 Corinthians 1:20

If you know that God has told you something, it doesn't matter when it was released—it has to come to pass. Your mentality should be: I'm going to maintain my position until I get what God has for me. By any means necessary, I have to get to the promise.

Therefore, my dear brothers and sisters, stand firm. Let nothing move you. Always give yourselves fully to the work of the Lord, because you know that your labor in the Lord is not in vain. —1 Corinthians 15:58

The ability to MAINTAIN your faith is a skill that requires much discipline and if mastered, will transform every area of your life. You have been given what it takes to maintain! Walk in it!

PRAY THIS PRAYER!

Lord, it's me again! You have given me what it takes to shake the nation! You have given me what it takes to operate in the fullness of my anointing! You have given me what it takes to reach my maximum potential in you. You have given me what it takes to live completely for you. You have called me forth for such a time as this to let your kingdom come and your will be done on earth as it is in heaven. I understand, God, that the power of life and death is in my tongue. I speak to my generation right now in the name of Jesus and I call forth a generation of young people who aren't afraid to live for you. God, I'm asking that you stir up the spiritual gifts amongst your people.

Give us total spiritual authority.

Help us to learn how to be bold in the gifts that you have given us. The devil has tried to keep us quiet for too long, but no longer will we negotiate with him. No longer will we compromise who we are, whose we are, and our assignment to please the world. Any talents that you have given us that we can use to advance the kingdom, we stir it up now. God, you have graced us in many areas of our lives. Help us not to live in a box and keep our talents quiet and enslaved to the opinion of the enemy. You made us and everything about us in your image. So everything we have and do is to glorify you. Receive our offering, God, because we give it back to you.

God, I'm praying to see you connect me with people who desire you more than they desire the things of the world. I'm looking for divine connections in this season. Connect me with people who can propel me into my destiny. Keep me away from anybody who is not sent by you. Transform my thoughts and break down my perceptions so I can receive everything you have for me in this season of my life. There have been many times in my life that I have missed what you were trying to do in me, but I'm declaring now that I won't miss you anymore.

Because of my hunger for you, I'm transitioning. Whatever you're doing in this season, don't do it without me. I don't want to move without you. I don't want to talk without you. I don't want to go without you. I can't live without you. It's in you that I live, move, and have my being. Even now, as I'm praying, a new anointing is coming over my life and a new level of influence is coming over my life. There will be people who are going to want to know you, not because of me, but because of who you are and what you put in me. People who have never desired you before will want to encounter you in the name of Jesus.

I thank you, God, for freedom. Freedom from my past. Freedom from who I used to be. Freedom over stress. Freedom over financial stability. Freedom over the opinions of others. Freedom over depression. Freedom over suicide. Freedom over my family. Freedom over any addiction.

I get it now, God! Because of you dying on the cross for my sins, I AM FREE! Even in the times where it doesn't look like I'm free, remind me of my freedom. And now that I'm free, I can be me! I don't have to hide who I really am. I can do what you called me to do. My purpose is clear now. My assignment is set before me now and it's all because of you. Give me the strength, God, to never return back to who I was. Give me strength to be bold and free. Let my light shine before others, that they may see your good deeds and glorify you in heaven. All I want to do is be pleasing in your sight. I'm ready! In Jesus' name I pray. Amen!

Made in the USA
Columbia, SC
13 May 2025